The **OCPD Basics**

Study **G U I D E**

Relationship **Restoring**

– The **Companion** *book*

In Question and Answer Format

for *Speedier* Comprehension

and Retention

By Mack W. Ethridge

OCPD Specialist, NFHR, Inc.

Copyright © 2020

By Mack W. Ethridge

Published by **New Frontier Health Research, Inc.**

Cover design by Mack W. Ethridge

Library of Congress Cataloging-in-Publications Data, Ethridge, Mack W.

The OCPD Basics Study Guide, Relationship Restoring – The Companion book

1st Complete Softback Edition, Jan. 2020

Table of Contents

<u>Vibrant Hope! – Conquering Your OCPD Tendencies</u>

Insight! Your Door to a Brighter Tomorrow!

The Many Detrimental Mindsets of the OCPD Person

Liberating, Truth-Laden Messages for the OCPD Person

New Book Announcement! When OCPD Meets the Power of God!

<u>Escaping Another's OCPD Tyranny!</u>

Telling Another They Have OCPD

The Golden Guiding Principle

Third-Party Approach to OCPD

How to Deal with an OCPD Person's Personal Appearance Upset

The Hidden, Yet True Opponent, in Your Encounters with an OCPD Person

The Peril that Must be Recognized and Decisively Acted Upon

Table of Contents – *Con.*

The OCPD Wife and Her *Often* Disastrous Impact upon *Both* the Marriage Relationship and Her Motherly Obligation

The OCPD Wife and Her *Often* Disastrous Impact upon *Both* the Marriage Relationship and Her Motherly Obligation **(quick view table)**

The OCPD Husband and His *Often* Disastrous Impact upon *Both* the Marriage Relationship and His Fatherly Obligation

The OCPD Husband and His *Often* Disastrous Impact upon *Both* the Marriage Relationship and His Fatherly Obligation **(quick view table)**

Declarations of God's Truth Over OCPD: Reinforcement Cards (9 different topic sets of 10 cards each) (*Available only in Parent volume*)

Declarations of God's Truth Over OCPD: The Central Golden Key

Farewell Message (to Source Volume)

Finis

Disclaimer

All instructions or recommendations in this book are not in any fashion to be construed as medical advice, either for physical, psychological, or mental ailments. This research paper is not intended to diagnose the existence of OCPD, nor to prescribe treatment. Nor is it meant to professionally analyze the mental health condition or emotional fitness of the OCPD person. In short, this book is meant for information purposes, only. Before putting into practice any of its ideas or concepts, you would be well-advised to consult a certified health professional conversant with these matters. Further, while these principles have proven effective for many individuals, the degree of success any <u>particular</u> OCPD person (or *other* person exhibiting a lesser number of OCPD traits), or non-OCPD person, may attain in utilizing the suggested recommendations is dependent upon a multitude of factors, including, but not limited to: the OCPD/non-OCPD person's level of intelligence, psychological state, personal temperament, physical condition, determination to succeed, and skillfulness in application of the principles. The author disavows any responsibility for the reader's use or misuse of any part of this work.

Author Qualifications

Mack Ethridge is a professional writer/researcher/ educator, who has devoted thousands of hours to the study of Obsessive-Compulsive Personality Disorder, and draws upon his *first-hand* observations of this disorder in action. He has pioneered methods and techniques of how the OCPD person may best obtain **Insight** into their disorder, and thereby, pave the road to their recovery. Lastly, Mack has *personally witnessed* the ongoing heartache and trauma of a distant relative suffering from their OCPD disorder, and *experienced* the terribly relationship-crippling characteristics of OCPD behaviors by this distant family member over a period of several years. And through this Research Report, he seeks to equip those OCPD people who suffer from this disorder with the beginning prerequisite knowledge and tools necessary for them to progressively become free of all its detrimental, health-harming, and interpersonal relationship assaulting compulsions; and for the <u>non</u>-OCPD person 'victim', this book will serve to begin to change their 'victim status' to that of a confident, **invulnerable strongman** or **woman** before the now-useless and ineffective attacks against their person by the OCPD person.

STUDY GUIDE

A Personal Letter

from the Author

<u>*Who* are the **intended audience** for this book?</u>

The intended audience for this book are the *non-*OCPD person and the person who suffers from OCPD (*preferably* with a <u>measure</u> of Insight!)

<u>What is the **overall** reason *why* this book was compiled</u>?

To address various ***initial*** (and subsequent) **aspects** of the OCPD phenomenon

<u>*Though* this book is not *explicitly* addressed to romantic couples, how is it that it **still** has **direct** bearing upon couples?</u>

It has direct bearing upon couples as it provides a *beginning framework* of highly relevant questions and solid answers germane (relevant) to the OCPD condition and situation

<u>What *types* of couples can benefit from this book?</u>

The types of couples that can benefit from this book are married couples, domestic partners, male/female housemates, and boyfriend/girlfriend coupled arrangements

<u>What is the *overall* **intention** of this book? What is it designed to ***accomplish***?</u>

This book is intended (meant) to *lay the groundwork* for both parties in romance (the OCPD person, *and* their loved one) to mentally and emotionally grow together as a couple

<u>*What* is this book designed to **prepare** the OCPD person and their spouse or loved one *for*?</u>

This book is designed to **prepare** both parties *for* more detailed, sophisticated knowledge and techniques required to become master over the OCPD phenomenon – and to neutralize its threat

<u>What ***platform*** of *presentation* does this book utilize to launch further study into the means and methods of conquering this formidable foe?</u>

The *specific* platform of presentation this book utilizes to launch further study into the means and methods of conquering this formidable foe are (1) a **starting approach** (utterly basic) to, and (2) a **crucial '*ABC*' understanding** of OCPD

<u>What is the *central* **disclosure** of this book?</u>

The central disclosure of this book is the knowledge of *how* to **banish** OCPD from lovers'/couples' consciousness and their shared lives

<u>What is the intended **joint** aim of this book's message?</u>

The intended joint aim of this book's message is to **educate <u>both</u> the novice** and the **intermediate learner** (especially couples) about the *real* issues at stake between them – by presenting life-saving, relationship restoring, psychologically-sound transformational Truths

<u>These guideposts (this book), *if recognized,* foreshadow a couples' **what**?</u>

These guideposts, once recognized (and *correctly* implemented) foreshadow a couples' **healing!**

Dedication

<u>What is the *primary* **motivation** underlying all of the OCPD person's thoughts, speech, and actions?</u>

The *primary* motivation underlying all of the OCPD person's thoughts, speech, and actions is the OCPD person's commitment to living a life of ***uncompromising*** excellence.

Author Qualifications

<u>How can I have **confidence** that the author of this book speaks with *genuine* authority that can be trusted?</u>

I can have confidence that the author of this book speaks with genuine authority that can be trusted because perhaps more so than anything else, he has devoted *thousands of hours* to the study of Obsessive Compulsive Personality Disorder, and draws upon his first-hand observations of this disorder in action.

(See <u>Author Qualifications</u>, above, for an extensive biographical sketch of the author's achievements and accomplishments.)

Vibrant Hope! – Conquering OCPD Tendencies

STUDY Insight! – **Your Door to a Brighter Tomorrow!** **GUIDE**

Gift Edition No. 1

<u>What is the **Principal** component required to conquer OCPD tendencies?</u>

The principal component required to conquer OCPD tendencies is the acquisition of INSIGHT, that elusive yet **critical** element necessary to view one's self realistically and truthfully.

<u>What is the *Wonderful* Thing about Insight that is so reassuring to the OCPD bound person?</u>

The Wonderful Thing about **Insight** that is so reassuring to the OCPD bound person is that by your paying attention to it, pondering and reflecting upon it, *consistently*, it tends to grow, opening the door to further OCPD deliverance 'revelations' and 'Aha' moments.

<u>What is the entire, **central** focus of the 'Only Hope' deliverance textbook this Study Guide refers to?</u>

The entire, central focus of the 'Only Hope' deliverance textbook this Study Guide refers to is that with faithful and _habitual_ reading, reflection, practice, and more practice, the OCPD person will begin to 'undue' those mental thought patterns (obsessions, or _strongholds_) and behavioral activities (compulsions, or _slave actions_) which have so hindered you from enjoying your life, and prevented you from appreciating those persons around you.

<u>Just what precisely **IS** Insight, and what relation, if any, does it have to Intuition?</u>

Insight has to do with the ability to _discern_ or _perceive_ the Truth of a matter. It involves <u>grasping</u> the true nature or **Reality** of a situation. It usually entails careful and accurate analysis or diagnosis of a major interest, problem, difficulty, or challenge. Although, at times, the **Truth** of a given scenario may be arrived at through intuition, or a 'flash' of understanding. Yet, either way, Insight affords an individual a **comprehension** that is in total alignment with the **Facts** of what is _really_ transpiring, becoming plain and self-evident to the bearer of Insight.

<u>What does it *mean* to be 'set free through Insightful Truth'?</u>

To be set free through Insightful Truth means, in the context of OCPD, that with every glimmer of Insight, each recognition of yours, *to yourself*, of the many ways in which YOU are sabotaging your precious life, creating unhappiness, and misery, and discontent, that you ACKNOWLEDGE (which is to say, **pause** to become aware of), you become *that <u>much</u> more free* to discard false viewpoints and to cease from carrying out detrimental behaviors. (Specific examples are provided in the Relationship Restoring book.)

<u>*Why* should you keep your 'Only Hope' textbook close at hand?</u>

You should keep your Only Hope volume close at hand – on your nightstand, on the corner of your home desk, in your briefcase, or in your automobile so that it will be *<u>readily</u> <u>available</u>* when you should need it for encouragement and frequent review throughout your day, and by doing so, you will soon find the grip of OCPD on your person *lessening* day by day – as you *relinquish* more and more attitudes of demandingness, criticalness, complaining, and perfectionistic ways of thinking.

<u>What will be the **outcome** of your adhering to the thoughtful admonishments and wise directives of the Only Hope volume</u>?

The **outcome** of your adhering to the thoughtful admonishments and wise directives of the Only Hope volume will be your liberation from a *tightly constricted* life of worry, unhappiness, discontent, and tormenting fear. No longer will you be a slave to these taskmasters, but, instead, you will come into your own <u>authentic</u> **personal power** to live your life to the full!

<u>What *other*-author mental health book does New Frontier Health Research *enthusiastically* endorse, and *why*</u>?

The other-author mental health book that New Frontier Health Research enthusiastically endorses is called ***'I Am Not Sick, I Don't Need Help!'***, 10th anniversary edition, by Dr. Xavier Amador (available through Amazon online). And we encourage our readers/students to obtain this book as it speaks *directly* to the challenge of patients acquiring Insight in order to lead a richer, fuller, more rewarding life. It literally is a masterpiece of wisdom one cannot afford to be without.

What is the *importance* of your setting your clear **Intention** to uncover your 'blind spots' relative to OCPD on *a daily basis*?

The importance of your setting your clear Intention to uncover your 'blind spots' relative to OCPD on a daily basis is that, over time, you WILL experience those *flashes* of awareness that will inform you of the **harmfulness** of your thoughts and actions, providing you with **strong incentive** to alter those thoughts and modify those actions to the benefit of all parties concerned.

What should you, an OCPD person, *do* when you experience inner upset, a disturbed disposition, or a lack of peacefulness?

When you experience inner upset, a disturbed disposition, or a lack of peacefulness, you should **pause**, and *thoughtfully* consider whether or not you are in the grip of an OCPD manifestation. This will allow for Insight to 'intervene', and for you to find relief from distress, and – for you to grow.

<u>What will your **Commitment** to alter your life for the better *entail* – relative to actions you **MUST** take to conquer the OCPD menace in your life?</u>

Your commitment to alter your life for the better relative to actions you **must** take to conquer the OCPD menace in your life entail deep soul-searching, a fearless honesty with yourself, and a <u>*ruthless*</u> (**<u>no</u>** pity or soft-hearted) scrutiny and analysis of those thoughts you entertain in your mind, on a recurring basis. It requires **training** your mind to recognize and to <u>*abandon*</u> erroneous, detrimental, contrary-to-Reality thoughts (and their associated hurtful and life-diminishing feelings) and to **embrace** accurate, mental-health engendering, *faithful*-to-Reality thoughts that will support you, strengthen you, and cause you to – in a wonderfully freeing and beautiful state of psychological freedom – to TRULY LIVE!

<u>What should you *continually* remind yourself of in your efforts to become free of OCPD?</u>

You should continually remind yourself in your efforts to become free of OCPD that you are <u>*deserving*</u> of experiencing a life of enjoyment, satisfaction, fulfillment, well-being, inner peace,

gratifying purpose, and rewarding accomplish-
ment, *regardless* as to the demerits of your past
beliefs, speech, actions, or behaviors. You did the
best you knew how at the time. Remind yourself,
you **ARE** a child of the Universe, a son or daugh-
ter of Life, Itself! You are on a NEW PATH now!
You, dear friend, are on the Road – *to Victory*!

Vibrant Hope! – Conquering OCPD Tendencies

STUDY **The Many Detrimental Mindsets of the OCPD Person GUIDE**

Gift Edition No. 2

<u>What does it *mean* that a person has 'full-blown' OCPD?</u>

A person who has full-blown OCPD possesses its characteristic dysfunctional traits to a *severe* and *maximal* degree. These dear people who are wholly 'possessed' by the OCPD mentality have **'zero'** amount of **Insight**, which means they have <u>*no*</u> conception **they** are the **CAUSE** of their own misery and torment.

<u>How can **you** know, for **certain**, that there is *considerable* hope for YOU to break free from the shackles of OCPD which now so limit and diminish and distress your precious life?</u>

You CAN know, for certain, that there IS <u>considerable</u> hope for you to **break free** from the shackles of OCPD which now so limit and diminish and distress your precious life because of your **willingness** to read this newsletter commentary, and your **longing** to self-evaluate yourself with accuracy, objectivity, and detachment. This, alone, PROVES you possess the necessary degree of Insight to *consciously* cultivate liberating attitudes, dispositions, and mindsets.

<u>What **ONE** word, perhaps more than *any* other, best describes the OCPD person?</u>

The one word that best describes the OCPD person is the word, **'unteachable'**. This overarching characteristic speaks to their utter obstinacy, or stubbornness, to believe others have anything of value or truthfulness or even trustworthiness to teach them for their benefit – this in spite of <u>*overwhelming*</u> evidence to the contrary! – disclosing their irrationality, lack of logic, and immature (undeveloped) thinking processes, patterns and perceptual interpretations.

<u>For the OCPD person who possesses a *measure* of Insight, **what** should they deliberately remind themselves of – on a **periodic** basis, and *why*?</u>

The OCPD person who possesses a measure of Insight should deliberately remind themselves on a periodic (recurring) basis the fact that, in all likelihood, they have a _propensity_ to be **unteachable**. And, that by recalling this harmful trait to mind, they can 'nip it in the bud' when it seeks to 'rear its ugly head' into one's thinking and feeling worlds.

<u>What harmful OCPD mindset goes _hand-in-hand_ with their unteachableness?</u>

The harmful OCPD mindset that goes hand-in-hand with their unteachableness (their unteachable _spirit_) is the mindset that **rejects** sound, viable, answers – and practical, workable solutions to their problems and difficulties, **outright**. Whether those problems be of a health nature (physical), psychological (mental/emotional), financial, relational, occupational, or spiritual. Consequently, they _never_ reap the benefits of the many remedies available to them.

<u>What affirmation can **best** address, and **overcome** objections to, the OCPD person's _predisposition_ to reject answers and solutions to their problems?</u>

The affirmation that can *best* address, and overcome objections to, the OCPD person's predisposition to reject answers and solutions to their problems is for them to recite (audibly, or in their mind) **'I am WILLING to <u>try</u>!'** – New things! Different things! Even unlikely things! Even things I'm <u>*disinclined*</u> to try! Recognizing <u>*those*</u> may be the **very** answers/solutions I seek!

<u>Why do countless OCPD people *momentarily* 'reflect' upon any given positive or hopeful suggestion *offered by another*, ONLY to **quickly** discard it</u>?

Countless OCPD people momentarily 'reflect' upon any given positive or hopeful suggestion offered by another, only to quickly disregard it, because the *longer* they should reflect, the *greater* their anxiety becomes.

This is so because their acceptance of it would show them to be <u>mistaken</u> in their evaluation of a given situation, if not outright **wrong**. And the mere thought of *being* wrong is simply <u>unbearable</u> to them! Consequently, they often exclaim, *'I don't want to think about it!'* Locking in failure.

<u>For those OCPD people who CAN see through the fallacy of refusing to *self*-examine, *self*-observe, and to *self*-reflect, what can they DO to demonstrate their receptivity to a pro-offered idea by another?</u>

For those OCPD people who CAN see through the fallacy of refusing to self-examine, self-observe, and to self-reflect, they can then *give themselves* **permission** to <u>adopt</u> another's suggestions as their own, and **incorporate** those suggestions into their daily activities in order to **prove** their effectiveness and validity. *If* proven to be <u>non</u>-solutions, one is still free to discard them, and to try something else.

<u>What is the **great hindrance** to the OCPD person (and to those about him) of 'circular thoughts' and 'cyclical conversation'?</u>

The great hindrance to the OCPD person (and to those about him) of 'circular thoughts' and 'cyclical conversation' is that their rehearsing a problem over and <u>over</u> again, focusing on the problem, <u>takes</u> <u>precedence</u> <u>over</u> taking ACTION to resolve the problem, and initiating possible solutions. Their expressed thoughts consist of unending 'loops' (to use computer language), going around and around in circles – always ending up where they started with _no_ perceived options, _no_ possible answers, and _no_ probable solutions.

<u>What is **'blindness'** to the _ultimate degree_ when it comes to an OCPD person observing, evaluating, and judging another</u>?

Blindness to the ultimate degree when it comes to an OCPD person observing, evaluating, and judging another is when the OCPD person _clearly_ sees any number of character faults in their fellow-woman or -man, but are **totally oblivious** to the FACT that they possess the <u>very same fault</u>, and more often than not, in a _much_ more pronounced way.

(This vital concept is further elaborated upon in **The Relationship Restoring OCPD Fundamentals** volume.)

What **powerful** tools can be adopted, and utilized, by the OCPD person to '*renew* their minds', and to *cause* them to become *ever-the-more* aware of **Life's Great Laws** governing their human relations and their happiness?

The **powerful tools** that can be adopted, and utilized, by the OCPD person to 'renew their minds', and to cause them to become ever-the-more aware of **Life's Great Laws** governing their human relations and their happiness are those **Truth Statements**, or affirmations, which, when faithfully used, establish a <u>confident</u> mental viewpoint exhibiting one's **Innate Authority** and **Victorious Power** over the OCPD enemy.

Ten, *Scientifically*-designed, 'Power Thoughts (actually, topical paragraphs) to Overcome OCPD' follow in the Relationship Restoring book, along

with ten 'Protecting my Mental Health' affirmations, as well. Just below are one example of each:

'I am **convinced** it is entirely possible for me to
overcome my OCPD tendencies in a relatively
short period of time. And, I realize I have
compelling reasons to do so. I recognize that I
have what it takes to succeed. And I _**WILL**_
succeed!'

'Today, I will experience the **many benefits** of
mental health ideals and practices when
interacting with my fellow-woman and -man. This
means I will extend to them a **highly respectful**
stance regarding _their_ autonomy and _their_
obligation to exercise it.'

<u>Why is it that the OCPD person does _NOT_ have to
believe all of the Truth Proclamations for them to
be _effective_ in their lives</u>?

The OCPD person does NOT have to believe all of
the Truth Proclamations for them to become
effective in their lives because with _committed_
reading and reciting of them _every_ day you will
COME to believe them, particularly as you begin
to experience more of the wellness and the
deliverance you seek in your internal state of
being. That internal gauge which registers how

happy, or how sad you are. How at peace, or how in distress you are. You will find your faithful reciting of them, with _**feeling**_, _**emotion**_, and _**emphatic**_ _**(forceful)**_ _**utterance**_ (this is important!), will positively 'color' whatever you subsequently think, say, or do. And your day will be an increasingly more enjoyable one, devoid of the OCPD 'drama' created by your own lack of Life-Enhancing knowledge.

Vibrant Hope! – Conquering OCPD Tendencies

STUDY Liberating Truth-Laden Messages for the OCPD Person **GUIDE**

Gift Edition No. 4

<u>What will the OCPD person's **consistent** *application* of the psychologically-sound – and powerful, Truth-laden Messages, presented, herein, most assuredly, bring about in their lives</u>?

The OCPD person's consistent application of the psychologically-sound – and powerful, Truth-laden Messages, presented, herein, most assuredly, will bring about in their lives **harmony**, **cooperation**, and **joy**, such as they have never known before; *especially*, as they are resorted to in conjunction with the study of the author's OCPD's Only Hope of Psychological Wellness deliverance volume, as each reinforces the other, and illuminates the other.

Ten *Scientifically*-designed, *'Fostering Accurate Self-Image'* affirmations (topically formulated paragraphs), are provided in **The Relationship Restoring book**, along with ten *'Ensuring Health*

Through True Thought' affirmations, and ten *'Valuing Relationships Above All'* affirmations. Examples of each topical section follow:

Fostering Accurate Self-Image

'I can feel *utterly* safe and *wholly* secure in knowing that others' talents and gifts are *not* a threat to me. In fact, I can **rejoice** in their good fortune, and I do! I **renounce** the errant thought that I am <u>diminished</u> in their presence, and instead feel **great pride** in them.

Ensuring Health Through True Thought

I can become a dynamo of **physical vibrancy** to an *ever-increasing* degree as I <u>one-by-one</u> let go of anger, attempts to control, criticize, complain, judge, be perfectionistic, or engage in useless worry. For with **physical stamina** and bodily **strength**, I can optimally function.

Valuing Relationships Above All

I set my **intention**, today, to account the *quality* of my relationships as *more* important than winning arguments, offering unsolicited advice, or verbally 'correcting' supposed mistakes of others. I **resist** these compulsions by seeing 'through' them to their harmfulness.

I recognize, at last, the advisability of allowing other people **their right** to make mistakes, the freedom to try things their _own_ way, the personal liberty to experiment as _they_ see fit. As **I** would **most certainly want** the *same* consideration – extended to me.

Vibrant Hope! – Conquering OCPD Tendencies
STUDY   New Book! **When OCPD**
Meets the Power of God!   **GUIDE**
Special Announcement Edition

<u>How does the author's new book **When OCPD Meets the Power of God** *differ* from his previous deliverance textbooks on OCPD, and What *advantage* does this afford the OCPD person?</u>

The author's new book When OCPD Meets the Power of God differs from his previous deliverance textbooks on OCPD in that it offers perspectives *fundamentally* different from his former work entitled OCPD's Only Hope of Psychological Wellness addressed *solely*, and compassionately, to the OCPD sufferer. The distinction between the two books involves them being written with both the OCPD sufferer, in mind, *and* the non-OCPD person who interacts with the OCPD person, as well.

This work approaches the subject of the mental illness of Obsessive-Compulsive Personality

Disorder from the viewpoint of the realm of invisible Spirit – *taking into account the originating Sources of either helpful Insight, or harmful influence, therefrom, whether for good or for ill.*

While each book presents information and knowledge that is indispensable to the OCPD person if they ever hope to regain, or acquire, their mental and emotional wellness, the latter publication cited above focusses upon the **psychological** aspects, whereas this newly-released publication concentrates principally upon the **spiritual** aspects.

That is why <u>both</u> books come highly recommended to the reader as they complement each other to a 'tee', and serve to reinforce each other in a dovetail fashion. So though it is true that OCPD people are being healed and liberated from OCPD slavery through their conscientious study of ***OCPD's Only Hope***, and their consistent application of the principles, techniques, and special knowledge provided therein (thanks be to God!), there almost certainly will be some instances where <u>*only*</u> the knowledge provided in **When OCPD Meets <u>the</u> <u>Power</u> <u>of</u> <u>God</u>**, and the faithful application of that knowledge, will be the catalyst for a more speedy and permanent deliverance, at last.

In short, **Insight** is investigated to a depth never before done, relative to its exact nature, its presence or absence, blocks to its entrance, sources of its coming, what _inhibits_ its emergence, or **_what allows it to flourish_**. The answers may surprise you, but it is The Truth that will set men free!

And, lastly, learn what the 'most learned', even the skilled researchers, do <u>not</u> know about OCPD due to _THEIR_ lack of **Insight** relative to the vital mental/spiritual component they either disbelieve, deny, or are fearful to even entertain, or investigate.

<u>Little Known Facts about the Author Affording You **Confidence**</u>

<u>in His **Credentials** and Qualifications to *Authoritatively* **Address** and **Set Forth Solutions**</u>

<u>to the Ever-Proliferating (when untreated) OCPD Disorder Challenge</u>

Mack Ethridge is uniquely qualified as no other person alive today to author '**When OCPD Meets the Power of God!**', as he is America's premier OCPD lay expert, having written the world's first and *only* comprehensive textbook and original, innovative workbooks on Obsessive Compulsive Personality Disorder, supplying his best-selling treatment and recovery volumes to the North Shore/Long Island Health Care System in New York.

He is also a leading expert on little-known, also new and restored, specialized aspects of Biblical knowledge (concerning our astounding Identity in Christ, claiming our Freedom in Christ, exercising our Authority in Christ, and, perhaps most importantly, obtaining the deliverance available through Christ, at every level of our beings, including mental/emotional/psychological, as well as spiritual); Whose books are in the private libraries of such world notables as Professor N.T. Wright (New Testament scholar and prolific best-selling author), Andy Andrews (prolific, best-selling author and inspirational speaker), Claire Pfann (Dean and New Testament Instructor at the University of the Holy Land in Jerusalem), Marilla Ness (the United Kingdom's leading Christian recording artist), Akiane Kramarik (America's child prodigy poet and painter), Tony Robbins (life coach and best-selling author of *Unlimited Power* and *Awaken the Giant Within*), and Pastor Joel Osteen (who needs no introduction). And he heads the Mercy Rose Ministries Worldwide Outreach, in operation, now, a decade and a half, as its Founder and Operational Director.

And with profound, scholarly Insights into the psychological makeup and inner motivations of OCPD people, arrived at through *thousands of hours* spanning a number of years, of research, ongoing direct, intimate contact, interaction with, and keen observation of OCPD persons, and Mack's intensive decades-long heart search into the spiritual depths of authentic Biblical Christianity, Mack stands wholly unequalled among OCPD researchers, writers, and instructors, as well as clearly unmatched among Christian ministers, teachers, and counselors, in his ability to convey Vital, life-freeing practices, disciplines, and Truths to OCPD people in the capacity of Master Teacher and Christian Scholar/Counselor, par excellence!

This *one-of-a-kind* psycho-spiritual combination of knowledge, skills, and heavenly communication gift of Mack's, so expertly synthesized, has produced a volume destined to become a trailblazing classic in the annals of OCPD Hope for Healing messages and Practices, and Illuminated Philosophy, for the OCPD person to safeguard and preserve their new-found, or rather newly-bestowed, Freedom and Deliverance, and <u>Victory</u>, from Above – *<u>at long last</u>!*

Escaping Another's OCPD Tyranny!

STUDY **Telling Another They Have OCPD GUIDE**

Gift Edition No. 1

<u>How can I tell this person who is a dear friend, colleague, or relative of mine, I believe they have a mental health problem – *without* their taking **offense**, feeling **insulted**, or becoming **alienated** from me</u>?

I can tell this person who is a dear friend, colleague, or relative of mine, that I believe they have a mental health problem – *without* their taking offense, feeling insulted, or becoming alienated from me by observing several **critical approach factors** which will 'set the stage' for the OCPD person to be *receptive* to my genuine concern for their welfare.

These all-important factors include:

1) Approach (as a caring friend <u>vs</u>. an accusing bystander)
2) Choice of language (affirming and conciliatory <u>vs</u>. provocative)

3) Setting (relaxed and quiet _vs_. distracting or disruptive)

4) Attitude (of genuine interest and support _vs_. 'you're on your own')

5) Suggestion ready (name and contact info. to a psychologist or psychiatrist, _both_ a male and a female, preferably)

(A detailed exploration of each of these factors is presented in The Relationship Restoring OCPD Fundamentals book for your thorough comprehension, and subsequent implementation.)

<u>What _further_ instructions may well be given on how **best** to tell the OCPD person of your heartfelt concerns about their welfare relative to OCPD</u>?

Some further instructions which may well be given on how best to tell the OCPD person of your heartfelt concerns about their welfare relative to OCPD are as follows: First, schedule your 'sharing' session with the OCPD person at a time of their convenience, where the two of you can comfortably sit down together, will not be disturbed, and where there will be no interruptions (turn off cell phones and/or mute the land-line). Perhaps the two of you could dine out together, in a comfortable and relaxed setting, and afterward, could broach the subject of their disorder, but not necessarily mention the name of their disorder (or even that it IS a disorder). Be sure that the OCPD person is in a fairly good mood at the time. Then, start out by thanking her or him for their coming, *reassuring* this person of your care and concern for their well-being, and of your appreciation for them. This is the best place to start!

(A full-fledged discussion scenario is thereafter presented in The Relationship Restoring OCPD Fundamentals book for your complete understanding relative to critical *language phrases* to use.)

Is there a Principle of Interaction that stands out **above all the rest** which should be observed when dealing with an OCPD person, which will afford the most **immediate** *'gain'* to the non-OCPD person, in terms of maintaining one's peace of mind *and* domestic tranquility?

The Principle of Interaction that stands out above all the rest which should be observed when dealing with an OCPD person, which will afford the most **immediate** *'gain'* to the non-OCPD person, in terms of maintaining one's peace of mind *and* domestic tranquility IS the Principle of **refraining** from responding to the OCPD person immediately, but, *instead*, reflecting 3 to 5 times *longer* than you normally would, before offering a statement or asking a question, prior to your speaking it.

This observance is a **_very_ fundamental** 'rule of engagement' that, *if* you are not careful, you will not give due consideration to; thereby, forfeiting, the protective benefit it invariably imparts.

Your adopting of THIS one principle of interaction (actually, **THE** _primary_ 'rule of engagement') with an OCPD person, _alone_, will save you untold moments and hours of grief and regret! This is so because prior to speaking **anything** to an OCPD person, you should pause long enough to ask yourself whether or not what you have to say will serve as a **trigger** to their automatic, dysfunctional, negativistic replies, and then reflect upon the likelihood of that happening. Below is the concept in brief reminder form, as it bears repeating:

The **Golden Guiding** Principle

<u>Before</u> responding to an OCPD person, reflect 3 to 5 times _longer_ than you normally would,

on your statement or answer (or question) – **prior** to your speaking it.

(You'll be <u>_SO_</u> **glad** that you did!)

This time of pausing and reflection may extend anywhere from **30 seconds** to <u>**several** minutes</u>, depending upon the nature, relevance, and possible 'volatility' of the topic you intend to introduce. If you are _pressed_ for a quick answer, respond by saying 'No, I wish to give careful consideration to your question before I speak. You, sweetheart [husband/wife], are worth that!'

(This vital topic is developed further in The Relationship Restoring OCPD Fundamentals book to illustrate its great importance, along with added recommendations on how *best* to implement.)

<u>What is the *best* antidote to my constant worrying over my loved one's OCPD condition, and the fears of our relationship steadily deteriorating, which so often intrude into my mind?</u>

The best antidote to my constant worrying over my loved one's OCPD condition, and the fears of our relationship steadily deteriorating, which so often intrude into my mind, consists of a two-part answer: (1) Become **aware** you are in a mental worrying 'mode', and then (2) **pause** sufficiently long enough to remind yourself that *your worry is a traitor to your cause*, that of your overall well-being and welfare.

A **key**, liberating thought is:

Worry is a <u>*useless*</u> pastime, offering **no** real benefits

Due to old habit thought patterns, you will initially feel this is not true. 'Does not worry cause me to explore the problem,' you ask yourself, 'and search for a solution?' **No**, it really does <u>not</u>. Worry consumes your precious life energy masquerading as a benefactor, causing you to *repeatedly* imagine all of the bad things that are 'sure' to occur.

Once you recognize this, you can **decide** to stop ruminating over your situation or challenge (as does a cow unceasingly chewing its 'cud', or regurgitated food), and instead make up your mind to take <u>physical</u> ACTION (*doing* something) to either alleviate, or to remedy, the situation. Sitting around and just 'thinking' about the problem is a sure recipe for mental and emotional turmoil!

Ponder your options, **yes**, consider your alternatives, **Yes**, evaluate what recourse is available to you, **YES**! But, do <u>not</u> dwell on the 'pros and the cons' too long. Set a *time limit* during which you can ponder the problem, then turn your attention to some *other* entirely different matter. If you wish, you can come back to your 'worry time' – later, and resume! This will help you to break this bad habit, in time. The following is <u>part</u> of a meditation concluding this Golden Guiding edition:

Worry is the Great *Self*-Betrayer

I now Know worry is my greatest enemy. It seeks
to discourage and frighten me into believing **the lie**
that preoccupation with a problem is mandatory.
Confidence an answer exists, is the antidote. How
deceptive is worry! It tries to convince me I should
become apprehensive, uneasy and afraid that so
and so will happen, or that such and such will
occur, or that I will not be able to handle it. It
never tells the Truth! **The fruitless exercise** of
worry would have me dwell upon what *might*
happen, what *could* happen, or 'worst case' scenar-
ios. I maturely consider all possible outcomes, but
I stay focused on solutions and answers.

I remind myself always that worry is a clever
adversary that stealthily sneaks into my mind if I
am not careful. It tries to demoralize and terrify me
with its unending recital of impending woe. I am
NOT fooled. **I condition my mind**, <u>*daily*</u>, to recite
and rehearse Truth statements, affirmations, and
poetic verities, which strengthen my thinking
processes to accept only a Vision of my Life that is
Whole and Growing. . .

Escaping Another's OCPD Tyranny!

STUDY   Third-Party Approach to   OCPD   GUIDE

Gift Edition No. 3

<u>What are the advantages of having a mutual friend broach the topic of OCPD to the person, my loved one, who has OCPD?</u>

The advantages of having a mutual friend broach the topic of OCPD to the person who has OCPD (your wife, husband, fiancé, etc.) are that the OCPD person _may_ be more **open** to (1) reflecting upon the idea further, and discussing it later with their friend, or (2) the OCPD person _may_ be more **willing** to speak to a counselor about the _possibility_ of their having it, not necessarily a psychologist or a psychiatrist, and/or (3) at least be **willing** to read literature (either an article or a book) that describes this condition, and ponder its relevance to themselves.

Now, WHY, in particular, might there be more of an openness and/or a willingness to do this? The following explains:

There was a saying once voiced by a man of wondrous wisdom, 'A prophet is _not_ without honor, save [except] in his own country, and in his own house [or household, relative to his influence there].' By extension, this principle could be applied to say, perhaps, a husband or wife, where one of the two has OCPD, and the other (the 'prophet', or the one who bears an unwelcome message) would seek to inform that loved one of their mental health condition. Of course, most often, the mentally ill person would view their concerned loved one 'without honor' (with some exceptions). That is to say, without _respect_ for what their spouse had to say, or, in other words, without _credibility_. For after all, as they see it, 'This is _just_ my husband speaking,' or 'This is _just_ my wife speaking.' 'No one especially qualified to make such an extraordinarily, even ridiculous, pronouncement – as if they were an authority on mental health issues!'

<u>What is **_actually_** happening in these instances where the OCPD mate gives little, or _no_, credence to their loved one's concern that they (their OCPD mate) suffer from it?</u>

What is actually happening in these instances where the OCPD mate gives little, or no, credence to their loved one's concern that they (their OCPD mate) suffer from it is, unfortunately, the **dynamic** of _interpersonal familiarity_. This dynamic involving such daily, close, life-interacting familiarity between two family members may well have lessened (even eroded) the high regard one would normally have for the other, which should be maintained between two related people, if harmony and goodwill are to prevail.

Of course, beyond this is the bigger challenge, which is lack of (or, _poor_) **'Insight'**, the technical, medical term being **anosognosia**. (Discussed at length in the author's ground-breaking volume entitled, 'When OCPD Meets the Power of God!'.)

Where can you find additional, authoritative, _extremely_ helpful and encouraging thoughts on the Nature of Insight available _anywhere_, today (apart from NFHR's courses of instruction)?

In Xavier Amador's landmark book, _I Am Not Sick, I Don't Need Help!_ – 10th anniversary edition (available through Amazon.com), Dr. Amador lays out a program of how to help someone with mental illness accept treatment. I highly recommend this book as probably the best book I have ever read on the topics he covers. It is truly an extraordinary book, born out of his decades-long interaction with his beloved mentally-ill brother, and his professional, life-long experience with mentally-ill patients as clinical psychologist and a professor of psychiatry at Columbia University New York City.

Even though the book deals primarily with schizophrenia and bipolar disorder, I can't recommend it more highly as he addresses issues such as denial, un-cooperation, effective interactive strategies, how to view and deal with the tremendous frustration and anger which can arise in yourself through contact with such psychologically impaired people, and how 'glimmers of Insight' are real cause for hope.

Further, Dr. Amador relates the most recent research (within the last few years) on the causes of poor Insight, and what can be done about it. And, finally, he originated an incredibly effective approach and method to interacting with the mentally ill person known as **L.E.A.P.** (Listen-**E**mpathize-**A**gree-**P**artner).

It has been tested and proven with hundreds of patients, and many of its principles are transferable to the OCPD context when used intelligently and with wisdom. Also, the concept of 'reflective listening' on the part of the non-mentally ill person is discussed in fascinating detail, and has proven to be a powerful tool for good.

For more information, visit
www.LEAPInstitute.org

<u>What are the predictable, *distressing,* results of an OCPD person (to *their* person) when not subscribing to (whole-heartedly *accepting*) the Life-Supporting Principle known as **'Intrinsic Worth'**</u>?

The predictable, distressing, results of an OCPD person (to *their* person) when <u>not</u> subscribing to (whole-heartedly *accepting*) the Life-Supporting Principle known as **'Intrinsic Worth'** is <u>very</u> low self-esteem which becomes very evident in their tone of voice, beliefs, and behaviors.

The concept of Intrinsic Worth has to do with worth *ascribed* to a human being for <u>*no other reason*</u> than that they ARE human beings – deserving of respect, dignity, and consideration.

One such statement often voiced by OCPD women is: 'I don't care what <u>*other*</u> people think about how

I look, but _I_ care!' This assertion will often follow a discussion you may have with her after she asks you (with great distress, or uncalled-for seriousness, evident upon her face) 'Do you think my hair looks alright?' or 'How do my eyes look – are they too puffy?' or 'Does this outfit make me look frumpy?' etc. And no matter what your reply, this dear person will immediately discount any positive, supportive statement you make, and she will insist that she does look 'a fright'!

Then, of course, you may have assured her that most people are _far_ too concerned about their _own_ interests and concerns and life that they hardly ever pay much attention to another's hairstyle, facial appearance, or state of dress. They may note it in passing, but they give it no further thought, and they certainly do not judge or condemn another for it! It is just not relevant to them. It has no impact upon their life.

Also, you may have told her that the majority of people routinely and automatically give allowance to others for _however_ they look, knowing that variation in grooming, the expression on one's face, or choice of clothing are all occasioned by many factors. Nothing to be worried over, or concerned about, ever. But, this, too, seldom works, and, unfortunately, falls upon 'deaf ears'.

So, what often happens when you say to the OCPD person there is really _no need_ to be concerned with what other people think (due to the above **true** rationale), she (or he) may even angrily say, 'No, as I said, I don't care what other people think about how I look, but I am concerned because **_I_** care about me!' But, of course, that is not true. For if the OCPD person **really** cared about themselves, that would take precedence over their appearance, and such a person would not upset and distress themselves over so small a matter (comparatively speaking) as appearance – over the far greater value of and desirability of fostering one's mental well-being. After all, it is not the appearance (good or bad) that confers **worth** upon a person, but the mere fact of their **personhood**, as a _unique_, distinct, _irreplaceable_ being made in the image of God.

It is the OCPD person's inability to make this crucial distinction that _self-condemns_ them to **fearful thinking** that they will appear undesirable, lacking in taste, stupid, or ignorant.

Given the above, be aware of this **faulty mindset** whenever your OCPD loved one or friend exhibits these speech patterns reflecting this aspect of a faulty thinking style. Do not attempt to convince her (through _repeated_ retelling), otherwise. Do not attempt (with _repeated_ effort) to show her the error of her thinking by telling her to do whatever she can, when she can, to 'fashion' her appearance as she may desire, and that there is no reason why she should trouble herself about this matter until such time and opportunity as she can make a change. She <u>will</u> <u>not</u> <u>listen</u>! Or, perhaps, better said, she <u>*wills*</u> not to hear!

The reality is she is simply <u>locked</u> into this misconception of herself, due to her OCPD condition, lacking the necessary **Insight** to see *through* or past this fallacy, which would free her from unnecessary distress, unease, and particularly painful self-consciousness.

And just remember, it is <u>not</u> your responsibility to convince her otherwise, and indeed, you **cannot** even if you try! This will spare YOU considerable distress by recognizing this. You may choose to disengage yourself from a conversation centering upon the OCPD person's appearance by simply saying:

'I like you [*or* love you] and value you <u>*any way*</u> you are.'

And, then, leave it at that. (Although you may need to repeat this statement until such time as the OCPD person discontinues her tirade.)

It is this 'unconditional acceptance' by you of their appearance that may, just _may_, in the long run, help this dear person to accept themselves, their humanity, and the 'perfect imperfection' all that implies! For one cannot look one's best at all times, nor is there any need to! – A simple fact of life.

Of course, the OCPD person's feelings are arising, too, from their mistaken belief that everything needs to be 'Perfect' (as _they_ define it) – especially their person! And, if not, they feel they become undeserving, as they have committed an _unpardonable_ sin! Bless them, God, in their ignorance! And increase _our_ patient bearing with them! – As well!

<u>What other _very_ distressing idea do many OCPD people dwell upon **continually** to their (and their listeners') detriment?</u>

The very distressing idea that many OCPD people dwell upon continually to their (and their listeners') detriment is the idea that they **must** be _terrified_ of the world, as a means, somehow, to protect themselves from it. Presumably, by being ever alert to the world's *imminent* menace *toward* them.

OCPD people, especially more so with women, often have an entrenched **'fear mentality'**. This fear begins with themselves (as with an <u>over</u>-concern with their appearance, as discussed above, fearing what other people *might* think of them) and extends to the whole world (as in all of the **horrible** and **unfortunate things** that are daily occurring to people in the world).

A number of these dear people will come right out and tell you, point blank, 'I am <u>terrified</u> of the world!', or 'Our government leaders are doing *nothing* about safeguarding our rights as Americans', or 'Our nation is going to be attacked and we are going to be made slaves!', or 'I am afraid of an imminent financial collapse!' And, on and on, it goes.

As in the first part of this issue, the same recommendation applies: It is best <u>not</u> to discuss these matters in depth with the OCPD person as their fear is unreasoning and reflexive. Even with reassurances to the contrary, the OCPD person will discount them and probably turn on you **accusing <u>you</u>** of not having a heart toward suffering people worldwide, or that you are being complacent about our national situation, or that there must be something terribly wrong with *you* not to get upset about all of this.

A helpful statement to recite to the OCPD person when this type of conversation is begun by them is:

'I am concerned about the welfare of others,

but *my* becoming upset will <u>*not*</u> help the situation.

It will only <u>add</u> to the fear and suffering of the world.'

Then, attempt to change the subject, or if need be, walk away from the OCPD person. For even attempting to persuade the OCPD person that so many of their concerns are unlikely to happen, or even if some of them did, they would be able to deal with it, will not quiet their fears, at all.

Again, it is the nature of their disorder to anticipate and see the worst! You can further say, **'I will do whatever is within my power to prevent any of these situations from occurring, but beyond that, I <u>refuse</u> to worry or fear.'**

Escaping Another's OCPD Tyranny!

The Hidden, yet *True Opponent*

STUDY in Your Encounters with an OCPD Person **GUIDE**

Gift Edition No. 5

<u>What will you have noticed (*if* you are keenly observant) when dealing with a close friend, a loved one, a relative, or a spouse, who has OCPD to an exasperating, if not infuriating degree, about what you are *actually* **witnessing** – playing out right before your eyes</u>?

What you will have noticed (if you are keenly observant) when dealing with a close friend, a loved one, a relative, or a spouse, who has OCPD to an exasperating, if not infuriating degree, about what you are actually witnessing – playing out right before your eyes, is that this dear person actually seems to be *'**possessed**'* by a power, an energy, or a force, if you will, that has them <u>*under its control*</u>. This 'something' is **compelling** them to act contrary to their own best interests, to foment strife and contention, and to generate the GREATEST disharmony, ill-will, and even aggression toward another. In short, to **destroy** healthful, life-affirming, beneficial, human- and God-honoring relationships.

Take the time to notice their facial expressions, and their eyes, *particularly*, which fairly proclaim their total immersion in, and/or captivity to, this 'field' of harmful and disruptive **Intention**.

Observe how this person is virtually reciting, in rote, *without* thinking, even as an automaton, words and concepts and viewpoints that are blatantly *illogical*, *nonsensical*, and *contrary to sound*, *healthful psychological principles* and *reality!* Notice how oblivious such an OCPD person is to this FACT, irrespective of whether you clearly, and *lovingly*, point this out.

Once you deliberately set out to do this mental observational exercise, and it only takes a few times, it is truly eye-opening; and most certainly is so, if you have never viewed it from this standpoint before.

Also, don't be surprised if you are a bit *startled*, as **Truth**, Life-Transforming **TRUTH**, often has a way of commanding a person's attention so that the message is powerfully conveyed to their consciousness to foster permanent mental retention for the good of the receiver.

Now, I'll repeat this, once more, as it bears repeating: It will become apparent, with careful observation, that this dear soul is _not_ acting rationally, is _not_ interacting sanely, and most assuredly is _NOT_ exercising their **free-will volition**, which would allow them: 1) to pause and _question_ their position, 2) _entertain_ different views, and, 3) _analyze_ the soundness of their position, or stance. It is as though these capacities _have been stripped from them_, leaving them helpless to propagate the **ill-intentions** and **ill-will** and **negative energies** of someone else, or _something_ else; again, all unbeknownst to their normal surface awareness.

It is as though a shroud, or a covering of some type, had been cast over their minds, **blinding** them to the harm and destructiveness they are spreading. And _if_ you, the non-OCPD person, have interacted only a _few_ times with an OCPD person who exhibits **full-blown** characteristics and traits, then you **KNOW** the above description is no mere exaggeration!

So, _what_ in Heaven's Name, is _actually_ transpiring here? The answer to this question, and there **IS** a definitive Answer, is that one can only entertain it, and accept it, _if_ you truly have an open mind, are an independent thinker, and possess a searching, fearless heart. Otherwise, **the Answer** will _forever_ elude you (as you will reject it), and the solutions you so earnestly seek will forever be beyond your mental grasp.

<u>What can be **categorically** stated, with *absolute* **certainty**, about the scenes you, as a non-OCPD person, are routinely witnessing, and enduring, the occurrences (particularly, those *bizarre, nonsensical* ones) that are playing out – right before your eyes</u>?

What can be categorically stated, with absolute certainty, about the scenes you, as a non-OCPD person, are routinely witnessing, and enduring, the occurrences (sometimes, even *bizarre*) that are playing out – right before your eyes IS that you are observing *<u>manifestations of the influence, direction, or even control of your loved one, by malevolent powers, intelligences, or entities</u>*.

I must hasten to add that these occurrences do NOT necessarily mean POSSESSION; in fact, in the **large majority** of the cases, it is <u>*not*</u>. Rather, these behaviors (even bordering on hostility) of OCPD persons are clear instances of **STRONG INFLUENCE** by what I call *<u>a Spirit of Anti-Life, Anti-Love, Anti-Good,</u>* and *<u>Anti-God</u>*!

The OCPD person, then becomes, an unknowing and unwilling (in the _sane_ part of their mind) **actor** or **pawn** – performing those actions which alienate the OCPD person to virtually anyone they come into contact with, and create mental and emotional havoc within their respective circles, such as professional, recreational, familial, etc.

<u>Should we ever be **fearful** of these ill-intentioned forces emanating from this malevolent Spirit of Anti-Life, Anti-Love, Anti-Good, and Anti-God?</u>

We _most_ definitely should **NOT** be fearful of these ill-intentioned forces emanating from this malevolent Spirit of Anti-Life, Anti-Love, Anti-Good, and Anti-God **because** those forces can exercise absolutely <u>NO</u> Power over us, _as long as_ we do <u>not</u> **nurture** or **nurse**, **foster** or **encourage**, **express** and **amplify**, within ourselves, as non-OCPD persons, the lower traits of human nature, such as anger, resentment, jealousy, envy, condemnation, criticism, hostility, negativity, and the like.

For it is _only_ when we, any human being, makes it **an <u>habitual</u> practice** to engage in these non-constructive and other-person disrespectful feelings, that the Anti-Life forces (whatever you conceive them to be) can **<u>add</u>** their negative energies to our own, ***amplifying*** them to greater, and *ever* greater degrees. Causing us (as OCPD persons are so prone to do) to spiral down deeper and *deeper* into an escalating vortex of depression, despair, dissatisfaction, and really, dangerous frames of mind in terms of one's mental stability, emotional health, relationship strengths, and overall life-adjustment, satisfaction, and fulfillment.

Which is all to say that the OCPD person, him- or her-self, is <u>NOT</u> your true antagonist, *not* your real opponent; but, rather, is the unfortunate and misguided **pawn** being used by that *something* other than themselves. That <u>*something*</u> which seeks their harm and demise.

For those who are <u>*not*</u> of the historic Christian faith, they may well call such a force an energy not understood or an unknown life-form coming from the <u>*para-normal*</u> realm. Not a supernatural realm, mind you, but **a dimension** science is just recently beginning to study and lend credence to. These respected, and fearless researchers, of high moral fiber and integrity, are called **parapsychologists**.

To the Christian, however, their Hebrew and Greek Scriptures make it abundantly clear, the propagation, and <u>*amplification*</u>, of the terribly distressing symptoms of OCPD people, are clearly in the province of **invisible**, **fallen** (relative to divine, or benevolent qualities) **beings**, and their involvement in the OCPD person's life is, without a doubt, a genuine reality. Such entities seem to _feed_ upon all such departures from love, and therefore have a vested interest in magnifying the same.

<u>What is **the Great Benefit** to the non-OCPD person in recognizing the _behind-the-scenes_ **Reality** of what is _truly_ transpiring, here, between their OCPD-enveloped loved one, and themselves?</u>

The Great Benefit to the non-OCPD person in recognizing the _behind-the-scenes_ Reality of what is truly transpiring, here, between their OCPD-enveloped loved one, and themselves is that the non-OCPD person can separate (in their minds and hearts) the poor, suffering OCPD person – from their harmful speech and behaviors, allowing one to *LOVE* them, the person; to *PITY* them, the person; and to have *COMPASSION* on them, the person; knowing that in a very real sense they are NOT responsible for their 'personality disorder'.

They have been insidiously taken over by something _beyond_ themselves. This realization brings a measure of **PEACE** to the non-OCPD person's heart who is forced to, or by loving choice determines to, interact with the OCPD captive. Such **Peace** as is so desperately needed by the _non_-OCPD person whose life is intertwined with the OCPD person whose very sanity has been ruthlessly and cruelly denied them, and their innate, divine qualities, suppressed within them.

May you, my fellow journeyer, on the path to a freer, fuller, more enjoyable life, independent of _any_ OCPD person's life situation, find <u>solace</u> in the above exposition, and an <u>encouragement</u> that will allow you to experience _more_ love toward the unfortunate OCPD person (though it may need to be at a distance), and _less_ negative feelings toward them as major disruptors of your life, and the lives of numerous others.

(Detailed, _extensive_, documented research on the above topic is available in the author's books entitled: **When OCPD Meets the Power of God!** and, **OCPD Bondage and Spiritual Warfare!**

These books provide the _EXACT_ methods and means to successfully **confront** these other-realm forces, enabling you to _lessen_ their influence, _curtail_ their activities, and even to ***banish*** their presence – from your loved one, and return your home to the <u>peaceful</u> <u>haven</u> it was meant to be!)

What **critically**-important acknowledgment is _seldom_ voiced by writers and researchers on the topic of OCPD to the **non**-OCPD person, _even from_ the safe distance of the written word?

The critically-important acknowledgment so _seldom_ voiced by writers and researchers on the topic of OCPD to the non-OCPD person, even from the 'safe distance' of the written word, is **what to do** when confronting an OCPD person who has FULL-BLOWN symptoms, with _zero_ Insight, and who possesses the **majority** (upwards to a dozen or so) of the disordered, negative, harmful, **primary** OCPD traits to a prominent degree. Those traits which so thoroughly identify and characterize the OCPD person.

These traits include: Controlling, criticizing, complaining, worrying, negative outlook, orderliness (extreme), perfectionistic (pathologic), rule bound, conscientious (to the absurd), discernment blindness (inability to differentiate) inflexible and rigid, judgmental (to the 'nth' degree), along with being aggressively demanding, highly argumentative, and blatantly disrespectful. Even to the point of angry, irrational 'persecution'.

So, we are <u>NOT</u> talking here about the clinically-diagnosed OCPD person who possesses only *three* or *four* of these traits (the minimum amount for a determination), which is problematic and distressing enough.

Rather, we are talking about the unfortunate soul who is ENVELOPED *by*, IMMERSED *in*, and wholly IMPRISONED *within* – the world of OCPD **madness**. And **Madness** (as in *severely* mentally ill) is the correct word. As there is simply no way to describe this situation 'delicately' or 'politely' if one is to convey the severity and seriousness of the matter, and to adequately impress upon the non-OCPD person the sheer ***'Fury'*** he or she may be facing!

This, perhaps, more than <u>*anything*</u> else, is the **greatest disservice** to the non-OCPD person as could be imagined. This includes professionals who either do not understand the **gravity** of the situation, or they **lack** the **courage** and **forth-rightness** to articulate it with clarity, conviction, persuasion, and power. (See the author's revealing book, **The OCPD Disorder, *Its True Seriousness and Unrecognized Peril!*** to protect yourself)

<u>What are the **five great evils** the OCPD wife *frequently* resorts to in her mis-guided attempts to get her own way?</u>

The **five great evils** the OCPD wife frequently resorts to in her mis-guided attempts to get her own way are: *usurping the authority of her husband, dishonoring her Creator, subverting her natural marital role, rebelling against her God-ordained purpose, and placing her children at risk of psychological disturbance.*

Now, Scripture makes it abundantly clear that the husband and his wife are 'heirs *together*' of the Grace of Life'. Both are unequivocally EQUAL in His sight relative to their importance, worth, and dignity, as 'bearers' of the Image of God. It is just that in God's Wisdom, He has assigned different roles to male and female to guarantee a harmoni-ous union, if only adhered to.

(These five evils are *thoroughly* explained and explored in **The Relationship Restoring OCPD Fundamentals** book, both through clear and concise narrative, as well as in a detailed <u>tabular presentation</u>, entitled *The OCPD Wife and Her Often Disastrous Impact upon Both the Marriage Relationship and Her Motherly Obligation.*)

<u>What are the **five great evils** the OCPD husband turns to in his mis-guided attempts to sadistically subjugate his family members</u>?

The five great evils the OCPD husband turns to in his mis-guided attempts to sadistically subjugate his family members are: *misusing his authority as husband, dishonoring his Creator, abusing his marital role, corrupting his God-ordained purpose, and placing his children at risk of psychological disturbance.*

Now, Scripture <u>*clearly*</u> places the **bulk** of the responsibility for the family welfare on the husband. He actually is *instituted* as the **'*king*'** (leader), **priest** (prayer warrior), and **prophet** (foreteller of good) over his family.

If he neglects any of these critical roles due to his OCPD sickness, he is harming his family, perhaps, irreparably.

(These five evils are *thoroughly* explained and explored in **The Relationship Restoring OCPD Fundamentals** book, both through clear and concise narrative, as well as in a detailed <u>tabular presentation</u>, entitled *The OCPD Husband and His Often Disastrous Impact upon Both the Marriage Relationship and His Fatherly Obligation.*)

Declarations

Of God's **TRUTH**

<u>*Over*</u> OCPD

THE CENTRAL GOLDEN KEY

I CAN and <u>*WILL*</u> become FREE of obsessive-compulsive tendencies and urges as I continually seek to acquire and expand my INSIGHT (Awareness, Perception, Comprehension) into the Great Laws of Life – *designed* for my greatest happiness and highest good.

<u>*For this*</u> **I AM Grateful!**
Amen!

Farewell Message

(to *Source* volume)

Dear OCPD Truth- and Relief-Seeking Friend,
This book has come to a close. You now know somewhat of the author's **dedication** to teaching others *how* to meet the assaults and abuses OCPD would impose on you, and how to, with determined resolve and effort, strip OCPD of its power to harm, and cause it to cease to be!

It is my heartfelt prayer that you have found something of value in this book relative to **bettering** your relationship with your loved one who either has OCPD, or is the party in your union who is the <u>non</u>-OCPD person. Either way, both of you suffer, and it is not right that you do! Nor is it necessary – that you continue to!

Therefore, for your relationship to be **reborn**, **grow**, and **flourish** as it was meant to, you will need every tool and armament at your disposal to confront your OCPD challenge, stand firm against it, and to permanently **defeat it!**

But, this can **ONLY** be done with accurate, detailed, specialized, scientific, yet *understandable*, knowledge, the very kind of knowledge (and practical advice formulated from it) the author has painstakingly sought out, researched, and compiled in layman's language so that *no one*, as long as they have a high school education, might find his material difficult to read or not understandable.

Or, worse yet, poorly presented, impractical, or ineffectual.

Now, then, is the time to **reread** this volume. Pause to reflect upon each passage, each instruction, each admonition. **Begin to put into practice** its recommendations, and *faithfully adhere to its outlined manner of engagement* with your OCPD loved one, or your non-OCPD loved one.

The future of you **as a couple** is at stake!

And, if this book makes sense to you, then by all means acquire other of the author's OCPD books, and LIVE the program!

It **<u>will</u>** work, *IF*, you **commit** to work it!

May it be so for you both!

With Every Good Mental Health Wish,

Mack W. Ethridge, President

New Frontier Health Research, Inc.

The **OCPD** <u>**Basics**</u> **Study G U I D E**

Relationship Restoring
– The **Companion** *book*

– Finis –

A New Frontier Health Research, Inc.,
Publication, Copyright © 2020